# EASTER PLANNER

# March

**NOTES**

# April

NOTES

# EASTER *Checklist*

## 1 MONTH BEFORE

- SET THE BUDGET
- CREATE GUEST LIST
- CREATE MENU
- PLAN DECOR

## 3 WEEKS BEFORE

- MAIL INVITES/NOTIFY GUESTS
- INVENTORY SUPPLIES
- CREATE SHOPPING LISTS
- BUY OUTFITS
- GATHER RECIPES

## 2 WEEKS BEFORE

- ORDER FOOD
- PURCHASE SUPPLIES/DECOR
- ORDER CAKE (IF NOT MAKING)
- GO SHOPPING

## 1 WEEK BEFORE

- FOLLOW UP ON RSVP'S
- BEGIN BAKING
- FINALIZE SHOPPING
- CREATE COOKING PLAN
- CLEAN THE HOUSE

## 1 DAY BEFORE

- SET THE TABLE
- FINISH BAKING
- CHILL BEVERAGES
- DECORATE
- SET OUT CLOTHES

## DAY OF

- COOK
- SPOT CLEAN
- GET READY
- ENJOY!

# EASTER *Planner*

| ACTIVITIES | DECOR | FOOD & DRINKS |
|---|---|---|
| | | |
| | | |
| | | |
| | | |

| PRIZES & FAVORS | TO-DO | NOTES |
|---|---|---|
| | | |
| | | |
| | | |
| | | |

## VENUE DETAILS

THEME:

DATE:

TIME:

PLACE:

# EASTER *Planner*

| ACTIVITIES | DECOR | FOOD & DRINKS |
|---|---|---|
| | | |

| PRIZES & FAVORS | TO-DO | NOTES |
|---|---|---|
| | | |

**VENUE DETAILS**

THEME:

DATE:

TIME:

PLACE:

# EASTER *Planner*

| ACTIVITIES | DECOR | FOOD & DRINKS |
|---|---|---|
|  |  |  |
|  |  |  |
|  |  |  |
|  |  |  |

| PRIZES & FAVORS | TO-DO | NOTES |
|---|---|---|
|  |  |  |
|  |  |  |
|  |  |  |
|  |  |  |

## VENUE DETAILS

THEME:

DATE:

TIME:

PLACE:

# WEEKLY *Agenda*

**WEEKLY PLAN**

- MONDAY
- TUESDAY
- WEDNESDAY
- THURSDAY
- FRIDAY
- SATURDAY
- SUNDAY

**TOP 3 GOALS:**

**TO DO:**

**TO MAKE:**

# WEEKLY *Agenda*

**WEEKLY PLAN**

- **MONDAY**
- **TUESDAY**
- **WEDNESDAY**
- **THURSDAY**
- **FRIDAY**
- **SATURDAY**
- **SUNDAY**

**TOP 3 GOALS:**

**TO DO:**

**TO MAKE:**

# WEEKLY *Agenda*

**WEEKLY PLAN**

- MONDAY
- TUESDAY
- WEDNESDAY
- THURSDAY
- FRIDAY
- SATURDAY
- SUNDAY

**TOP 3 GOALS:**

**TO DO:**

**TO MAKE:**

# WEEKLY *Agenda*

**WEEKLY PLAN**

- MONDAY
- TUESDAY
- WEDNESDAY
- THURSDAY
- FRIDAY
- SATURDAY
- SUNDAY

**TOP 3 GOALS:**

**TO DO:**

**TO MAKE:**

# WEEKLY *Agenda*

**TOP 3 GOALS:**

**WEEKLY PLAN**

MONDAY

TUESDAY

**TO DO:**

WEDNESDAY

THURSDAY

**TO MAKE:**

FRIDAY

SATURDAY

SUNDAY

# WEEKLY *Agenda*

**WEEKLY PLAN**

- MONDAY
- TUESDAY
- WEDNESDAY
- THURSDAY
- FRIDAY
- SATURDAY
- SUNDAY

**TOP 3 GOALS:**

**TO DO:**

**TO MAKE:**

# EASTER Menu

## APPETIZERS

- 
- 
- 
- 
- 

## MAIN DISH

- 
- 
- 
- 
- 

## SIDE DISHES

- 
- 
- 
- 
- 

## SOUPS/SALADS

- 
- 
- 
- 
- 

## DESSERTS

- 
- 
- 
- 
- 

## BEVERAGES

- 
- 
- 
- 
-

# EASTER *Menu*

## APPETIZERS
- 
- 
- 
- 
- 

## MAIN DISH
- 
- 
- 
- 
- 

## SIDE DISHES
- 
- 
- 
- 
- 

## SOUPS/SALADS
- 
- 
- 
- 
- 

## DESSERTS
- 
- 
- 
- 
- 

## BEVERAGES
- 
- 
- 
- 
-

# TO-DO List

# TRADITIONS & *Activities*

**TOP MUST DO'S**
- 
- 
- 
- 
- 

**THINGS TO DO:**
- 
- 
- 
- 
- 

**LET'S WATCH:**
- 
- 
- 
- 
- 

**THINGS TO MAKE:**
- 
- 
- 
- 
- 

**TO READ:**
- 
- 
- 
- 
- 

**PLACES TO GO:**
- 
- 
- 
- 
-

# TRADITIONS & Activities

**TOP MUST DO'S**

**THINGS TO MAKE:**

**THINGS TO DO:**

**TO READ:**

**LET'S WATCH:**

**PLACES TO GO:**

# EASTER *Guests*

| NAME | CONTACT INFO | # GUESTS | ✓ |
|------|--------------|----------|---|
|      |              |          |   |
|      |              |          |   |
|      |              |          |   |
|      |              |          |   |
|      |              |          |   |
|      |              |          |   |
|      |              |          |   |
|      |              |          |   |
|      |              |          |   |
|      |              |          |   |
|      |              |          |   |
|      |              |          |   |
|      |              |          |   |
|      |              |          |   |

# EASTER *Guests*

| NAME | CONTACT INFO | # GUESTS | ✓ |
|------|--------------|----------|---|
|      |              |          |   |
|      |              |          |   |
|      |              |          |   |
|      |              |          |   |
|      |              |          |   |
|      |              |          |   |
|      |              |          |   |
|      |              |          |   |
|      |              |          |   |
|      |              |          |   |

# EASTER *Guests*

| NAME | CONTACT INFO | # GUESTS | ✓ |
|------|--------------|----------|---|
|      |              |          |   |
|      |              |          |   |
|      |              |          |   |
|      |              |          |   |
|      |              |          |   |
|      |              |          |   |
|      |              |          |   |
|      |              |          |   |
|      |              |          |   |
|      |              |          |   |
|      |              |          |   |
|      |              |          |   |
|      |              |          |   |
|      |              |          |   |

# EASTER *Budget*

**PAPER GOODS**

| ITEM | BUDGET | ACTUAL |
|------|--------|--------|
|      |        |        |
|      |        |        |
|      |        |        |
|      |        |        |
|      |        |        |
|      |        |        |

**ENTERTAINMENT**

| ITEM | BUDGET | ACTUAL |
|------|--------|--------|
|      |        |        |
|      |        |        |
|      |        |        |
|      |        |        |
|      |        |        |
|      |        |        |

# EASTER *Budget*

**PAPER GOODS**

| ITEM | BUDGET | ACTUAL |
|------|--------|--------|
|      |        |        |
|      |        |        |
|      |        |        |
|      |        |        |
|      |        |        |
|      |        |        |

**ENTERTAINMENT**

| ITEM | BUDGET | ACTUAL |
|------|--------|--------|
|      |        |        |
|      |        |        |
|      |        |        |
|      |        |        |
|      |        |        |
|      |        |        |

# EASTER *Budget*

**MEALS/ BEVERAGES**

| ITEM | BUDGET | ACTUAL |
|------|--------|--------|
|      |        |        |
|      |        |        |
|      |        |        |
|      |        |        |
|      |        |        |
|      |        |        |
|      |        |        |

**DECOR/CRAFTS/PROJECTS**

| ITEM | BUDGET | ACTUAL |
|------|--------|--------|
|      |        |        |
|      |        |        |
|      |        |        |
|      |        |        |
|      |        |        |
|      |        |        |

# EASTER *Budget*

**MEALS/ BEVERAGES**

| ITEM | BUDGET | ACTUAL |
|---|---|---|
|  |  |  |
|  |  |  |
|  |  |  |
|  |  |  |
|  |  |  |
|  |  |  |
|  |  |  |

**DECOR/CRAFTS/PROJECTS**

| ITEM | BUDGET | ACTUAL |
|---|---|---|
|  |  |  |
|  |  |  |
|  |  |  |
|  |  |  |
|  |  |  |
|  |  |  |

# EASTER *Budget*

**FOOD**

| ITEM | BUDGET | ACTUAL |
|------|--------|--------|
|      |        |        |

**MISC**

| ITEM | BUDGET | ACTUAL |
|------|--------|--------|
|      |        |        |

# EASTER *Budget*

**FOOD**

| ITEM | BUDGET | ACTUAL |
|---|---|---|
|  |  |  |
|  |  |  |
|  |  |  |
|  |  |  |
|  |  |  |
|  |  |  |

**MISC**

| ITEM | BUDGET | ACTUAL |
|---|---|---|
|  |  |  |
|  |  |  |
|  |  |  |
|  |  |  |
|  |  |  |
|  |  |  |

# EASTER *Budget*

**EASTER BASKETS**

| ITEM | BUDGET | ACTUAL |
|------|--------|--------|
|      |        |        |
|      |        |        |
|      |        |        |
|      |        |        |
|      |        |        |
|      |        |        |
|      |        |        |

**GIFTS/PARTY FAVORS**

| ITEM | BUDGET | ACTUAL |
|------|--------|--------|
|      |        |        |
|      |        |        |
|      |        |        |
|      |        |        |
|      |        |        |
|      |        |        |
|      |        |        |

# EASTER *Budget*

**EASTER BASKETS**

| ITEM | BUDGET | ACTUAL |
|------|--------|--------|
|      |        |        |
|      |        |        |
|      |        |        |
|      |        |        |
|      |        |        |
|      |        |        |

**GIFTS/PARTY FAVORS**

| ITEM | BUDGET | ACTUAL |
|------|--------|--------|
|      |        |        |
|      |        |        |
|      |        |        |
|      |        |        |
|      |        |        |
|      |        |        |

# TO-DO List

# TO-DO List

# EASTER *Baskets*

**CHILD:**

| ITEM | PRICE | BOUGHT |
|------|-------|--------|
|      |       |        |
|      |       |        |
|      |       |        |
|      |       |        |
|      |       |        |
|      |       |        |

**CHILD:**

| ITEM | PRICE | BOUGHT |
|------|-------|--------|
|      |       |        |
|      |       |        |
|      |       |        |
|      |       |        |
|      |       |        |
|      |       |        |

# EASTER *Baskets*

**CHILD:**

| | ITEM | PRICE | BOUGHT |
|---|---|---|---|
| | | | |
| | | | |
| | | | |
| | | | |
| | | | |
| | | | |

**CHILD:**

| | ITEM | PRICE | BOUGHT |
|---|---|---|---|
| | | | |
| | | | |
| | | | |
| | | | |
| | | | |
| | | | |

# EASTER *Baskets*

**CHILD:**

| | ITEM | PRICE | BOUGHT |
|---|---|---|---|
| | | | |
| | | | |
| | | | |
| | | | |
| | | | |
| | | | |
| | | | |

**CHILD:**

| | ITEM | PRICE | BOUGHT |
|---|---|---|---|
| | | | |
| | | | |
| | | | |
| | | | |
| | | | |
| | | | |
| | | | |

# EASTER *Baskets*

**CHILD:**

| | ITEM | PRICE | BOUGHT |
|---|---|---|---|
| | | | |
| | | | |
| | | | |
| | | | |
| | | | |
| | | | |
| | | | |

**CHILD:**

| | ITEM | PRICE | BOUGHT |
|---|---|---|---|
| | | | |
| | | | |
| | | | |
| | | | |
| | | | |
| | | | |
| | | | |

# EASTER *Baskets*

**CHILD:**

| ITEM | PRICE | BOUGHT |
|---|---|---|

**CHILD:**

| ITEM | PRICE | BOUGHT |
|---|---|---|

# EASTER EGG Hunt

| DATE | TIME |
|---|---|
| LOCATION | # PARTICIPANTS |
| # EGGS NEEDED | PRIZES NEEDED |

## EGG FILLERS/PRIZES

## ACTIVITIES/GAMES

# EASTER EGG *Hunt*

**DATE**

**TIME**

**LOCATION**

**# PARTICIPANTS**

**# EGGS NEEDED**

**PRIZES NEEDED**

## EGG FILLERS/PRIZES

## ACTIVITIES/GAMES

# EASTER EGG *Hunt*

| DATE | TIME |
|---|---|
| LOCATION | # PARTICIPANTS |
| # EGGS NEEDED | PRIZES NEEDED |

## EGG FILLERS/PRIZES

## ACTIVITIES/GAMES

# EASTER *Week*

## MONDAY

## TUESDAY

## WEDNESDAY

## THURSDAY

## GOOD FRIDAY

## SATURDAY

## EASTER SUNDAY

# EASTER Week

| MONDAY | TUESDAY | WEDNESDAY |
|--------|---------|-----------|
|        |         |           |
|        |         |           |
|        |         |           |
|        |         |           |

| THURSDAY | GOOD FRIDAY | SATURDAY |
|----------|-------------|----------|
|          |             |          |
|          |             |          |
|          |             |          |
|          |             |          |

### EASTER SUNDAY

# EASTER Week

| MONDAY | TUESDAY | WEDNESDAY |
|--------|---------|-----------|

| THURSDAY | GOOD FRIDAY | SATURDAY |
|----------|-------------|----------|

| EASTER SUNDAY |
|---------------|

# EASTER *Shopping*

## OUTFITS

- 
- 
- 
- 
- 

## GIFTS

- 
- 
- 
- 
- 

## DECORATIONS

- 
- 
- 
- 
- 

## ENTERTAINMENT

- 
- 
- 
- 
- 

## EASTER BASKETS

- 
- 
- 
- 
- 

## EASTER EGGS/FILLERS

- 
- 
- 
- 
-

# EASTER *Shopping*

## OUTFITS

- 
- 
- 
- 
- 

## GIFTS

- 
- 
- 
- 
- 

## DECORATIONS

- 
- 
- 
- 
- 

## ENTERTAINMENT

- 
- 
- 
- 
- 

## EASTER BASKETS

- 
- 
- 
- 
- 

## EASTER EGGS/FILLERS

- 
- 
- 
- 
-

# EASTER *Shopping*

## OUTFITS

- 
- 
- 
- 
- 

## GIFTS

- 
- 
- 
- 
- 

## DECORATIONS

- 
- 
- 
- 
- 

## ENTERTAINMENT

- 
- 
- 
- 
- 

## EASTER BASKETS

- 
- 
- 
- 
- 

## EASTER EGGS/FILLERS

- 
- 
- 
- 
-

# TO-DO List

# COOKING *Plan*

| TUESDAY: | WEDNESDAY: | THURSDAY: |
|---|---|---|
| | | |

| FRIDAY: | SATURDAY: | SUNDAY: |
|---|---|---|
| | | |

# COOKING *Plan*

**TUESDAY:**

**WEDNESDAY:**

**THURSDAY:**

**FRIDAY:**

**SATURDAY:**

**SUNDAY:**

# GROCERY *List*

| FRUITS | VEGETABLES | CANNED GOODS |
|---|---|---|
| | | |

| SPICES/OILS | DAIRY | MEAT |
|---|---|---|
| | | |

# GROCERY *List*

| FRUITS | VEGETABLES | CANNED GOODS |
|--------|------------|--------------|
|        |            |              |
|        |            |              |
|        |            |              |
|        |            |              |
|        |            |              |
|        |            |              |
|        |            |              |
|        |            |              |

| SPICES/OILS | DAIRY | MEAT |
|-------------|-------|------|
|             |       |      |
|             |       |      |
|             |       |      |
|             |       |      |
|             |       |      |
|             |       |      |

# GROCERY *List*

## DESSERTS

## SNACKS

## BEVERAGES

## BREADS/ROLLS

## OTHER

## OTHER

# GROCERY *List*

## DESSERTS

## SNACKS

## BEVERAGES

## BREADS/ROLLS

## OTHER

## OTHER

# TO-DO List

# EASTER *Recipes*

**RECIPE:**

**INGREDIENTS**

**DIRECTIONS**

**PREP TIME:**   **COOK TIME:**   **YIELDS:**

**RECIPE:**

**INGREDIENTS**

**DIRECTIONS**

**PREP TIME:**   **COOK TIME:**   **YIELDS:**

# EASTER *Recipes*

**RECIPE:**

**INGREDIENTS**

**DIRECTIONS**

**PREP TIME:**     **COOK TIME:**     **YIELDS:**

**RECIPE:**

**INGREDIENTS**

**DIRECTIONS**

**PREP TIME:**     **COOK TIME:**     **YIELDS:**

# EASTER *Recipes*

**RECIPE:**

**INGREDIENTS**                    **DIRECTIONS**

**PREP TIME:**          **COOK TIME:**          **YIELDS:**

**RECIPE:**

**INGREDIENTS**                    **DIRECTIONS**

**PREP TIME:**          **COOK TIME:**          **YIELDS:**

# EASTER *Recipes*

**RECIPE:**

**INGREDIENTS**　　　　　**DIRECTIONS**

**PREP TIME:**　　**COOK TIME:**　　**YIELDS:**

**RECIPE:**

**INGREDIENTS**　　　　　**DIRECTIONS**

**PREP TIME:**　　**COOK TIME:**　　**YIELDS:**

# EASTER *Recipes*

**RECIPE:**

**INGREDIENTS**                **DIRECTIONS**

**PREP TIME:**      **COOK TIME:**      **YIELDS:**

**RECIPE:**

**INGREDIENTS**                **DIRECTIONS**

**PREP TIME:**      **COOK TIME:**      **YIELDS:**

# COOKING *Timetable*

| MENU ITEM | COOK METHOD | READY TIME | COOK TIME | BEGIN COOK | PREP TIME | BEGIN PREP |
|---|---|---|---|---|---|---|
| | | | | | | |
| | | | | | | |
| | | | | | | |
| | | | | | | |
| | | | | | | |
| | | | | | | |
| | | | | | | |
| | | | | | | |
| | | | | | | |
| | | | | | | |
| | | | | | | |
| | | | | | | |

# COOKING *Timetable*

| MENU ITEM | COOK METHOD | READY TIME | COOK TIME | BEGIN COOK | PREP TIME | BEGIN PREP |
|---|---|---|---|---|---|---|
| | | | | | | |
| | | | | | | |
| | | | | | | |
| | | | | | | |
| | | | | | | |
| | | | | | | |
| | | | | | | |
| | | | | | | |
| | | | | | | |
| | | | | | | |

# EASTER *Photos*

PLACE YOUR EASTER
PHOTOS HERE

PLACE YOUR EASTER
PHOTOS HERE

# EASTER *Photos*

**PLACE YOUR EASTER
PHOTOS HERE**

**PLACE YOUR EASTER
PHOTOS HERE**

# EASTER *Photos*

**PLACE YOUR EASTER PHOTOS HERE**

**PLACE YOUR EASTER PHOTOS HERE**

# EASTER *Photos*

**PLACE YOUR EASTER
PHOTOS HERE**

**PLACE YOUR EASTER
PHOTOS HERE**

# EASTER *Photos*

PLACE YOUR EASTER
PHOTOS HERE

PLACE YOUR EASTER
PHOTOS HERE

# EASTER *Photos*

**PLACE YOUR EASTER
PHOTOS HERE**

**PLACE YOUR EASTER
PHOTOS HERE**

# EASTER *Photos*

**PLACE YOUR EASTER
PHOTOS HERE**

**PLACE YOUR EASTER
PHOTOS HERE**

# EASTER *Photos*

**PLACE YOUR EASTER
PHOTOS HERE**

**PLACE YOUR EASTER
PHOTOS HERE**

# EASTER *Photos*

**PLACE YOUR EASTER
PHOTOS HERE**

**PLACE YOUR EASTER
PHOTOS HERE**

# EASTER *Photos*

**PLACE YOUR EASTER
PHOTOS HERE**

**PLACE YOUR EASTER
PHOTOS HERE**

# Notes

# Notes

# Notes

# Notes

www.ingramcontent.com/pod-product-compliance
Lightning Source LLC
Chambersburg PA
CBHW081235080526
44587CB00022B/3951